My Life As A Service Dog!

As told by "Remarkable Maggie"

Recorded by Ellen Lenox Smith

www.wow-books.com

ISBN-13:
978-1537423234

ISBN-10:
1537423231

I dedicate this book

to my courageous master and mom,
Ellen Lenox Smith,
who wrote down the words of this book
as I barked them to her,

and her husband, Stu,
who taught me how to really serve
someone you love.

"Remarkable Maggie"

Woof woof!

Hi, my name is Maggie, and I am a black lab who was chosen to become a service dog. Do you know what that means?

A service dog is specially selected for months of intensive training with many different people that help, to teach us how to help people who can't do everything themselves.

Let me share my remarkable story with you.

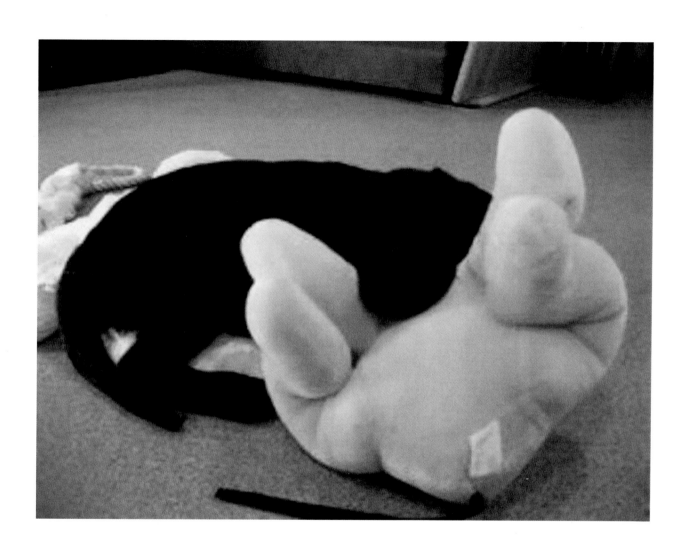

They picked me

First, experts picked me from a litter of puppies to be a service dog. They took me to my new home called NEADS (Dogs for Deaf and Disabled Americans) They saw my gentle personality and thought I would be the right puppy to train.

I lived there for four months, in the puppy house. I played in the backyard, which included a slide to go down! Trainers kept using the same commands, so I learned fast. For instance, I quickly learned "sit," "down," "stay," "leave it", and "hold." They were getting me ready for a very important job to do.

See how little I am right now?

Prison

When I was four months old, I was moved again to live, of all places, in a prison, where two kind prisoners trained me. For me, it was just two more kind people that were taking care of me and teaching me the commands I needed to learn to be able to help my future match. They had two men assigned to work with me instead of one since they didn't want me to get "bonded" yet. That special relationship was saved for who I was going to be matched with. I wonder who that person was going to be?

These are photos of my friend that was trained in a prison, like me. We slept right in their rooms and got lots of special attention. We practiced the commands we needed to know every day.

Foster home

On the weekends, I got used to a foster mom picking me up and bringing me home with her. She took me everywhere to prepare me for life as a service dog. We went to the ocean, rode on buses, trains, and subways. She even let me go swimming in the backyard pool, took me to the ocean and in the winter, I loved playing in the snow.

All my field trips and fun we had were helping me train for going anywhere and understanding how to be happy, behave and be helpful.

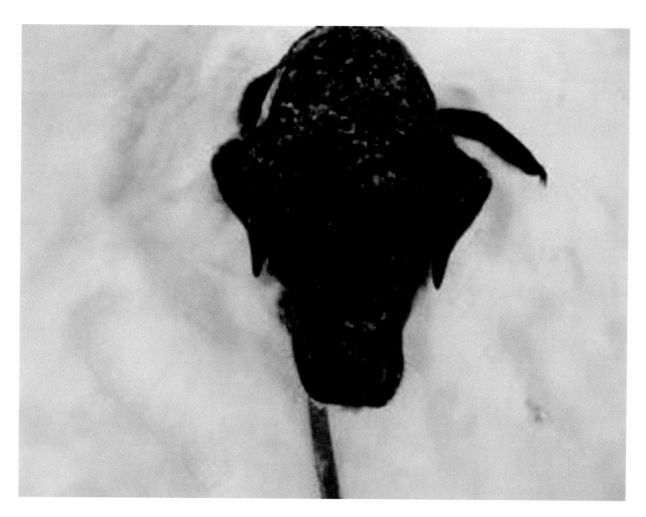

Me in the snow.

Final training

When I was one and a half, I was sent back to NEADS for my final training getting me ready to meet "my new mom." I could tell they were getting me ready for someone very special who needed me more than any other dog.

Look at how much I have now grown!

My new mom

Well, here she is. This person is Ellen, my perfect
match. She was skinny, wearing a big leg brace on her
poor leg, and was mostly using a wheelchair. It's easy
to please her, and it makes me proud, every time I do!

Hi, Mom!

Snuggling

This is Ellen and me the first time we snuggled on the bed at our NEADS training. We both sighed and fell asleep. I had never slept with a person on a bed before: now it's my new favorite! This is the life!

For two weeks, we work together so she could catch up to my skills in helping her. For instance, I show her I how good I am at opening doors, turning on lights, getting the phone, open handicap doors, retrieve medication or food from the refrigerator, and even barking on command. Oh yes, I have skills!

Light switches

Ellen can't believe how good I am at turning the light switch on and off at her command.

Opening doors

Ellen had a tough time learning to use the wheelchair and holding my leash, while I open the door for her.

Imagine that: I trained my mom!

This was one of the longest lessons before she started to get it right. It's so hard for her doing two things at once, but we repeated it over and over until we succeeded. We did it together!

We service dogs have to be patient with humans. They learn as we train them.

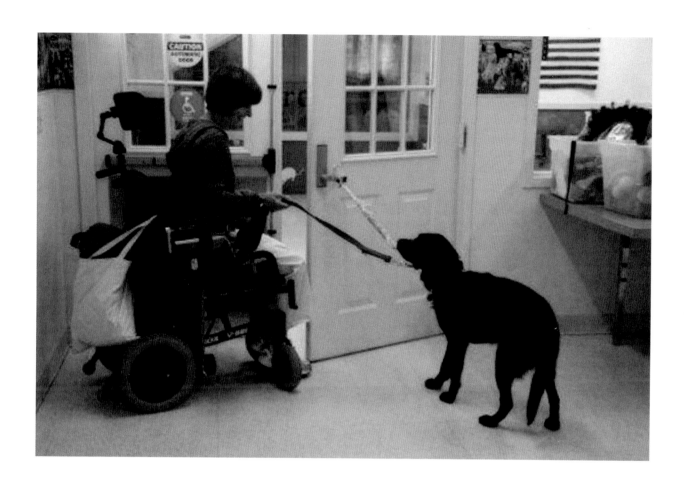

Waiting for commands

Here's one of my trainers who was trying to distract me, but I know that I have to wait for my commands! I am showing them that I listen to Ellen and not anyone else now unless given permission. I showed them all right! This one is easy compared to getting the door open.

Outside

We practice how to get around in the city with each other. Ellen always tells me "side," which is her command telling me to walk on her side. She uses hands signals too, so she can command me even if she can't speak.

See us out in public and "working." We get to wear our special red vests that let others know we are service dogs.

Restaurant

Towards the end of our training together, we visit a restaurant for practicing how to enter and exit, and for figuring out where I should lie down and wait. Guess where they put me? Under the table. It's a time of peace and quiet for me while Ellen visits. But, it is funny by the time we get up and leave, many people have no idea I have been under there! This is a good chance to show others how well remarkably behaved I am.

Handicap ramp

I also practice with Ellen on getting on and off the handicap van, as well as how to lay in a down position while we travel.

Time for love

When Ellen commands, "my lap," I jump up to snuggle with her. This task is the easiest of all.

Sometimes I sneak a kiss in... and she loves to give me a kiss too!

Almost ready to leave

At the end of our two-week training, my classmates and I go through testing to be sure we could stay together with our partners.

That's me on the far right. Notice how small I am compared to the others. Ellen needs a smaller dog to be able to invite into her lap in case she never walks again.

Meeting my new family

After two weeks training together at NEADS, I go home to live with Ellen for good.
All of Ellen and her husband's four sons, wives, and grandchildren quickly include me as part of their family. How lucky I am!

Do you see me in the front? I wonder where they would be without me in their lives?

Would you like to know more things I am doing for her now at home?

Refrigerator

Every morning and evening, I open the refrigerator, on command, to get her medicine pack. I hand it to her and then close the door.

One time, she forgot her medication when going to bed, so I sat in front of the refrigerator and would not come to bed until she remembered. This is my job! I never forget that this is the most important thing I do.

Doors and air mattress

I open all handicap doors for Ellen by being commanded to nudge my nose on the square button. Have you ever noticed those square buttons to press by a heavy door?

I also now know how to turn on and off her air mattress on her hospital bed. She used to forget to turn it on after taking her leg brace off and then would have to put it on all over again to get to the end of the bed to put the switch on.

Like I said, humans make so many mistakes and learn slowly. We service dogs have to be patient and train them.

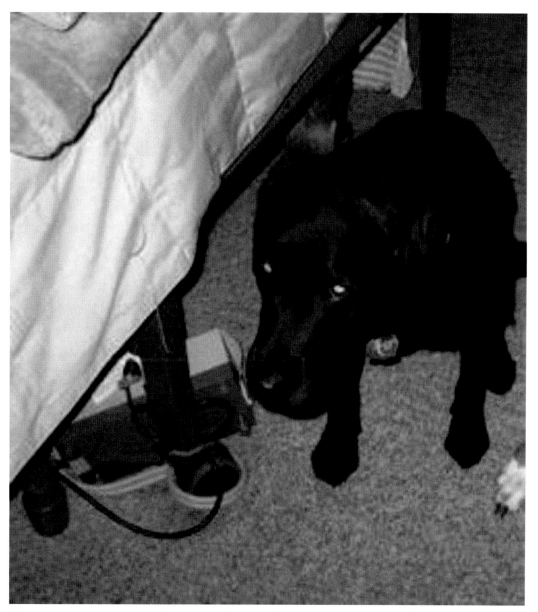

Here I am waiting for the command to turn on the air mattress. What a silly look on my face.

Breathing

When Ellen sleeps, she uses a breathing machine. When I had only been home for six days with Ellen, I realized she wasn't breathing on Thanksgiving morning. I licked her face and neck over, jumping onto the bed next to her. She eventually woke up, but she clearly didn't feel very well. Since then, I am invited to sleep next to her to keep her safe. Nobody taught me to do this. I just know when she needs to breath more by watching and listening to her, and then I go to work!

This is one of the many reasons they call me
"Remarkable!"

Appointments

I go with her and her husband Stu to physical therapy every week. Everyone is so nice to me there, and I love the attention they give me. They are like family to us all. On some of those days, we also attend doctor appointments.

I get to play with my buddy George sometimes when Ellen is having her Physical Therapy. I have gone to his school to teach the kids about service dogs.

Exercise

Many days, we go to the pool. I lie by the special hammock on pulleys called a Hoyer lift that lifts Ellen in and out of the water, like a crane. After she gets into the water, I lie down at the end of the lane.

Working

This is where I wait while Ellen is put into the pool. I keep an eye on her. If I sense she is not doing well, I get up and sit and stare at her to let know she needs to stop until she gets out.

Sometimes, people come over and pet me. Without my command to "SAY HELLO" from Ellen, I just ignore them. Once she gives me the command, I say hello to them. But I always remember to not greet anyone without the ok from Ellen. I am working!

I even carry her earplugs container. I would do anything for her!

Grooming

Afterward, I go into the handicap shower with Ellen and keep her company.

Every day, Ellen combs me and wipes my fur down with a damp cloth. It feels great and keeps me extra clean to be around the public. I also get my ears cleaned out and have my teeth brushed. I love all that attention!

Delivering

I go to the office and deliver the pool membership cards behind the counter. Then, when Ellen is finished at the pool, I go back to the office to get the cards back. Ellen says, "HOLD" and then "DELIVER."

People are so nice to me at the pool. They made me my own membership card with my photo on it! Can you believe they sang happy birthday to me on my birthday? Ellen and I had fun that day!

Playtime

My black lab puppy, Winston, comes over to play with me. I love running with him, and we have a terrific time exercising together. Ellen watches my weight carefully so I can keep to keep up him.

My friend is growing bigger than me, but I keep up with him even though I am now eight years old! Can you tell which one is me?

Train rides

I took a train ride with Ellen and visited Washington. I carried my food for four days in my red backpack, along with a ball and my favorite chew toy. We lived in a hotel for four nights, attended meetings, and visited the Capital. We met with both our Senators and Congressman. I was welcomed into each of their offices and even received a treat from the guards when first screening us.

This is me carrying the train tickets for Ellen. Can you see me? It is hard to see my black body against the dark floor!

Advocating

Here we are meeting Congressman Langevin at his office. Ellen's work is important. Still, I get bored with politics.

Demonstrating

I'm carrying a sign for Ellen at the State House, helping her at a demonstration.

Flying

I get to go on many plane rides, too.

This is me squished at Ellen's feet on the plane. Notice my big red vest. It is what I wear when we travel. The pockets hold all my food, my identification, and other needed supplies.

Many of our flights together have been for Ellen to have surgery. I am welcomed into the hospital. One time, we lived together there for 15 days. I slept on her hospital bed, went to rehab with her daily, and when she wasn't well enough to take me out, many people helped out.
The nurses thanked me for helping her. I made their jobs easier.

Parting

Here we are right before Ellen is taken away for her surgery. I stay with Ellen until the last minute before her surgery. I get pretty upset, but Stu, Ellen's caring husband, takes good care of me and brings me up to her room right after. Good thing I am patient!

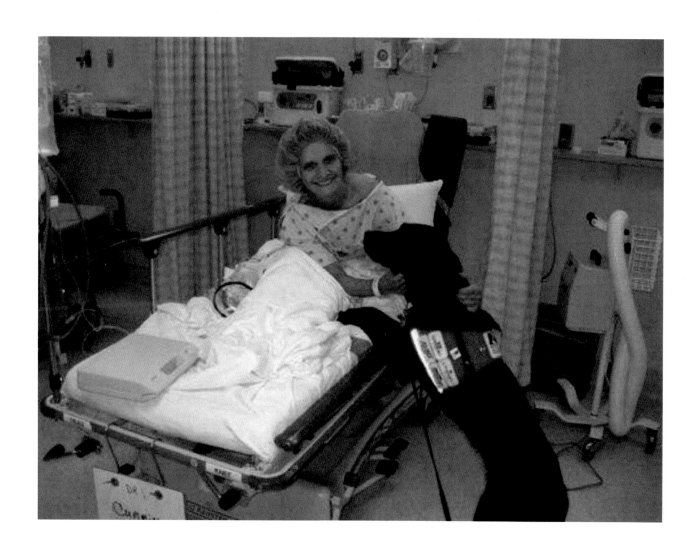

Back together again!

I am always excited to be reunited with Ellen, after surgery.

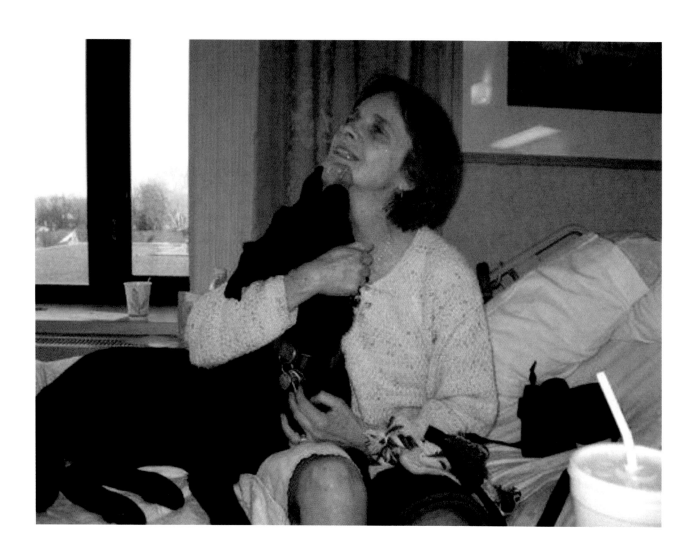

Nurse's assistant

I support Ellen's arm as the nurse takes blood. The nurse thanks me too!

Can you see why they call me ***"Remarkable*?"**

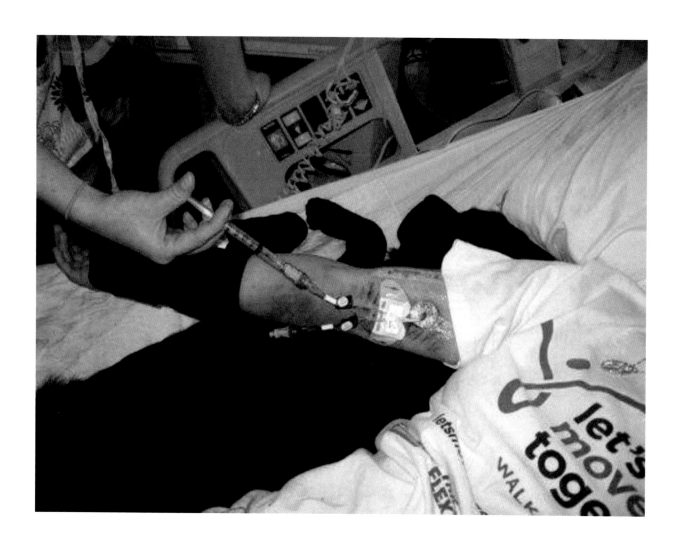

Warmth and pain relief

I give comfort and pain relief by lying against Ellen's body. This produces warmth and is called "spooning," like fitting together two spoons.

She is amazed at how much it helps her pain. She invites me onto her lap or bed when she is having a tougher day so she can get this remarkable help from me.

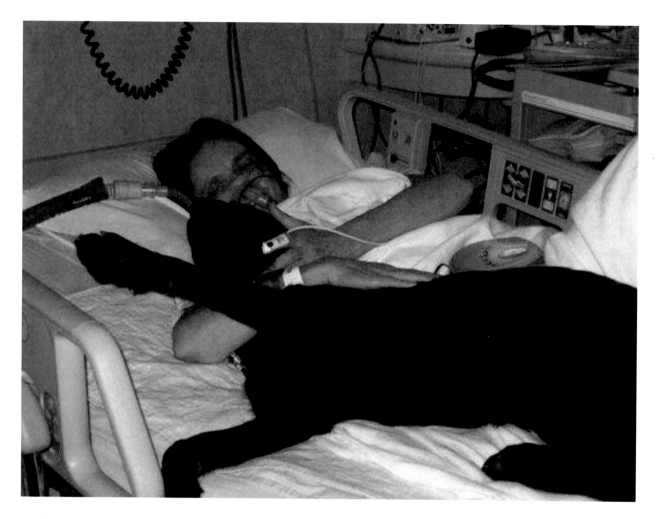

This is me "spooning" against my mom to help her to feel better.

Going home

We were both excited to be leaving the hospital and fly back home.

I am so happy I was selected to be a service dog. It feels good to be able to help others, and I feel so loved by Ellen, her family, and friends. Our life together is great!

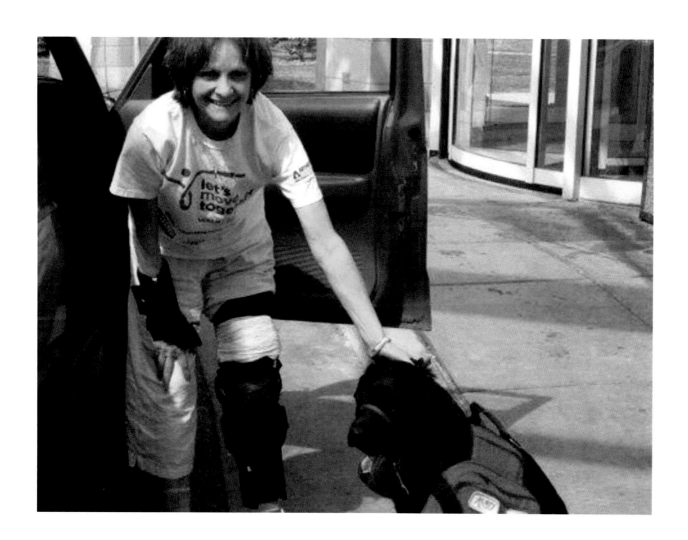

Best Friends!

Some wonderful people helped make this book wonderful:

- The amazing staff at NEADS, *(Dogs for Deaf and Disabled Americans)* who trained Maggie.

- Staff and inmates of Gardiner Prison, MA, generously helped us...

- My thanks to Rebecca Farnlof, the Arthritis Foundation Community Engagement Director for CT, MA, and RI, for her amazing advocacy.

- Thanks to, RI Congressman Langevin, for all his tremendous support for all we have ever requested of him.

- I appreciate editing by Pam Fracareta and Jillian VanNostrand.

**And I am grateful to all these lovely people--
and dogs--
who also contributed their love and
participation:**

- Erin Wylie, a puppy trainer from NEAD.

- My good friends: Karin Boyce and her dog Lucky,
  Wendy Foster and her dog Tippy.

- Eddie Vedro and Maggie's actual brother, Houdini, that
  trained with me to receive our dog.

- Some our family: our son Timothy and wife Shaina
  Smith and their son Landon; our son Christopher (wife
  Amy, missing); My husband Stu Smith, our son
  Benjamin Smith (wife Alison missing) and our son Ryan
  with his wife Cathleen and their son Henry (son Ronan
  missing).

- George Muldowney, Richard Califano and Betty Milazzo.

- And dear friend Pam Fracareta's dog, Winston.

Talk to Maggie!

I'd love to hear from you.

- How did you like my book?

- What story made you laugh?

- What picture made you want to be a service dog?

- What do you want to ask me?

Phone or email my mom, Ellen.

She will translate your human talk into barking.
Then I will understand and answer you.

Talk to Ellen!

I will happily connect you with Maggie.

I will bark out your message to her and send you back her response in plain English.

- **Call me:**
  401-474-0115

- **Email me:**
  ellen.smith2@gmail.com

Talk to me, if you want to hear my stories about being Maggie's mom and creating this book.

WOW! Books

creates an extraordinary tool for YOU

to formulate <u>your</u> personal insight
in just a few hours of your time
into a compelling, concise
experience
that you can share *powerfully*
with others.

To create a *WOW-Book* for yourself
Contact Nitsan Gaibel:
781-784-9960
www.WOW-Books.com

45372753R00044

Made in the USA
Middletown, DE
16 May 2019